10/4 5

Kansas
The Sunflower State

Jason Glaser

PowerKiDS
press.
New York

To the Blue Earth County Library, within whose walls much of this book was written

Published in 2010 by The Rosen Publishing Group, Inc.
29 East 21st Street, New York, NY 10010

First Edition

Editor: Amelie von Zumbusch
Book Design: Greg Tucker
Photo Researcher: Jessica Gerweck

Photo Credits: Cover © Philip Gould/Corbis; p. 5 © Gary Moon/age fotostock; p. 7 MPI/Getty Images; p. 9 Kean Collection/Getty Images; p. 11 © www.iStockphoto.com/Luther Zimmerman; p. 13 Randall Stotler/Getty Images; p. 15 © Larry Fleming/age fotostock; pp. 17, 22 (tree, animal, flag, flower) Shutterstock.com; p. 19 Carl Iwasaki/Time & Life Pictures/Getty Images; p. 22 (bird) © www.iStockphoto.com/Noah Strycker; p. 22 (Amelia Earhart) Sasha/Getty Images; p. 22 (Bob Dole) Chip Somodevilla/Getty Images; p. 22 (Martina McBride) Rick Diamond/Getty Images.

Library of Congress Cataloging-in-Publication Data

Glaser, Jason.
  Kansas : the Sunflower State / Jason Glaser. — 1st ed.
     p. cm. — (Our amazing states)
  Includes index.
  ISBN 978-1-4358-9395-5 (library binding) — ISBN 978-1-4358-9782-3 (pbk.) — ISBN 978-1-4358-9783-0 (6-pack)
  1. Kansas—Juvenile literature. I. Title.
  F681.3.G53 2010
  978.1—dc22
                                    2009029406

Manufactured in the United States of America

CPSIA Compliance Information: Batch #WW10PK: For Further Information contact Rosen Publishing, New York, New York at 1-800-237-9932

Contents

Home in the Heartland

Some people call Kansas the heartland of America. This is because Kansas sits at the very center, or heart, of the **continental** United States. Kansas is one of the Great Plains states. The Great Plains are in the middle of the United States. The plains are flat grasslands. Their earth is good for farming.

For thousands of years, Native Americans depended on the land's rich natural **resources**. Starting in the sixteenth century, many European and American travelers visited Kansas. Most saw the land's great openness as having no value and passed it by. In time, though, some of these travelers settled down in Kansas. They discovered the state's rich soil. The settlers grew food and founded towns. Soon, the land felt like home!

Thanks to its rich soil, Kansas is home to more than 60,000 farms. Since a lot of wheat is grown there, the state is known as the Breadbasket of the World.

Unwanted Land

The name Kansas comes from the Kansa, one of several Native American groups who lived in what would become Kansas. In 1541, Spanish soldier Francisco Vázquez de Coronado entered that area looking for gold. He found no gold and left after claiming the land for Spain. The Spanish traveled on horseback. In time, the Indians took up riding horses, too. They used horses for hunting, fighting, and traveling.

French fur traders reached Kansas by traveling on the Missouri River. Some stayed and claimed the land as part of French Louisiana. The land seemed worthless to the Spanish, so they did not argue over it. In 1803, France sold Kansas and the rest of French Louisiana to the United States.

This picture shows Coronado and his soldiers crossing Kansas. They were drawn to the land in search of the Seven Golden Cities of Cibola, where there was said to be much gold.

Bleeding Kansas

In the 1850s, many Americans moved to the Kansas **Territory**. Some wanted Kansas to become a state that allowed **slavery**. Others wanted Kansas to outlaw slavery. This time is called Bleeding Kansas because people on both sides were killed. People fighting against slavery were Jayhawkers. In 1856, Jayhawkers killed five slavery backers at Pottawatomie Creek, Kansas. They were mad that slavery backers had attacked Lawrence, Kansas, a town that opposed slavery.

In time, the Jayhawkers won. In January 1861, Kansas became a free state. People kept arguing about slavery throughout the country, though. In April 1861, several Southern states left the **Union** over slavery. This started the Civil War.

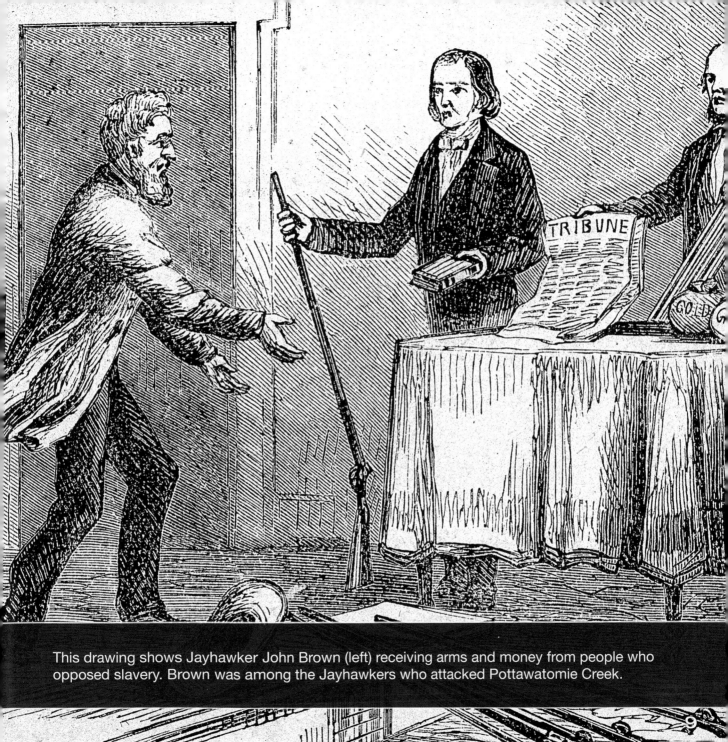

This drawing shows Jayhawker John Brown (left) receiving arms and money from people who opposed slavery. Brown was among the Jayhawkers who attacked Pottawatomie Creek.

As Flat as a Pancake

Kansas is made of very flat, grassy land called a plain. In eastern Kansas, where it rains the most, the grass grows taller. Tallgrass **Prairie** National Preserve, the largest tallgrass prairie in the United States, lies across the Flint Hills of eastern Kansas. In the western part of the state, the land sits a bit higher and there is less rain and shorter grass.

Spring can bring trouble in Kansas. Walls of air from both sides of the country meet overhead. Sometimes hot and cold air spins around together as **tornadoes**. The fast tornado winds are strong and can lift animals, people, or even cars! During dry years in the 1930s, winds blew huge dust storms across Kansas. The dust covered everything and made it hard to breathe.

Kansas is known for its wide-open spaces and the flatness of its land. In fact, the land there is so flat that people speak of the state as being as "flat as a pancake."

Life in the Grasslands

Many of the best-known animals in Kansas are small **mammals**. Foxes and coyotes prowl through the grass, scaring jackrabbits, squirrels, and prairie dogs into hiding. Ducks, geese, and red-tailed hawks fly across the blue sky. An eagle or buzzard might rest upon a red cedar, the only evergreen tree **native** to Kansas.

The American bison is the largest land animal in North America. It is also the Kansas state animal. Kansas was once home to many bison. However, most bison were killed by hunters in the nineteenth century. Today, there are no wild bison left in Kansas. You can see bison only in special parks. At Sandsage Bison Range, visitors watch bison chew on grass and imagine how Kansas once looked.

Female bison give birth to calves in the spring. The calves are big babies. They can weigh as much as 65 pounds (29 kg). Calves stay with their mothers for about a year.

Business Is Growing

Several kinds of wild sunflowers are native to Kansas. Farmers there also grow sunflowers as a crop. Sunflower seeds are made into many things, such as snacks, sunflower oil, and birdseed. Kansas raises so many sunflowers that it is called the Sunflower State. Soybeans and corn are also key crops in Kansas. However, the state's most important crop is wheat. Kansas farmers grow more wheat than farmers in any other state do.

If you have ever flown in a plane, at least part of it was likely built in Wichita, Kansas. Wichita builds more planes than any other city in the world. The **helium** that balloons use to get off the ground also may have come from Kansas. Helium, oil, and natural gas are all mined in Kansas.

Kansas is also home to many farmers who raise animals. This Kansas dairy farmer is caring for a newborn calf. Dairy farmers raise cows for their milk.

Welcome to Topeka

The importance of Native Americans to Kansas shows in Topeka, the state capital. A **sculpture** of an Indian pointing his bow and arrow into the sky stands atop the capitol building there. Inside the Kansas Museum of History, curious visitors can look at a Cheyenne tepee. You can also see the home of Charles Curtis in Topeka. Curtis was the only person of Native American background to become vice president of the United States.

Other visitors might like Topeka's Combat Air Museum. This museum has fighter planes in it that date back to World War I. Since the museum is on a real airfield, visitors often get to see Air Force and U.S. Army airplanes and helicopters in action.

The Kansas Senate and the Kansas House of Representatives meet in the capitol, seen here. These two bodies pass laws for the state. The state's governor has an office in the capitol, too.

Separate but Unequal

Though the state of Kansas never allowed slavery, African Americans there did not have the same rights as whites. For many years, African-American children had to go to different schools.

In 1951, Topeka parents who wanted all children to go to school together agreed to take the school board to court. When the U.S. **Supreme Court** heard the case in 1954, all nine judges agreed with the parents. They said that having different schools for children of different skin colors was against the law. Fifty years later, a school in Topeka was turned into the Brown v. Board of Education National Historic Site. It was named after the Supreme Court **decision** that outlawed having different schools for children of different races.

Linda Brown (first in the right row) was one of the children whose parents took the Topeka School Board to court. Their case brought about changes in schools across the United States.

The Cowboy Capital

Picture a cowboy riding through a town in the Old West. The town you are imagining most likely looks a lot like Dodge City, Kansas. From 1876 to 1885, cattle herders and bison hunters lived wild lives in lawless Dodge City. Famous gunfighters such as Wyatt Earp, Bat Masterson, and Doc Holliday had to come to bring order to the well-known town.

Though Kansas was once part of the Wild West, it is now a place that people are proud to call home. Many Kansans are proud of the University of Kansas. The school is known for its sports teams. Basketball star Wilt Chamberlain and football star Gale Sayers both played there. Who knows what stars Kansas will produce next?

Glossary

continental (kon-tuh-NEN-tul) Having to do with the 48 states in the United States that touch each other.

decision (dih-SIH-zhun) The ruling of a judge or group of judges.

helium (HEE-lee-um) A light, colorless gas.

mammals (MA-mulz) Warm-blooded animals that have backbones and hair, breathe air, and feed milk to their young.

native (NAY-tiv) Born or grown in a certain place or country.

prairie (PRER-ee) A large place with flat land and grass but few or no trees.

resources (REE-sawrs-ez) Things that occur in nature and that can be used or sold.

sculpture (SKULP-cher) A figure that is shaped or formed.

slavery (SLAY-vuh-ree) The system of one person "owning" another.

Supreme Court (suh-PREEM KORT) The highest court in the United States.

territory (TER-uh-tor-ee) Land that is part of a country but is not a state or province.

tornadoes (tawr-NAY-dohz) Storms with funnel-shaped clouds that produce strong, spinning winds.

Union (YOON-yun) The group of states that together make up the United States.

Kansas State Symbols

State Tree
Cottonwood

State Animal
American Bison

State Flag

State Bird
Western
Meadowlark

State Flower
Native Sunflower

State Seal

Famous People from Kansas

Amelia Earhart
(1897–1937)
Born in Atchison, KS
Aviator

Bob Dole
(1923–)
Born in Russell, KS
Politician

Martina McBride
(1966–)
Born in
Medicine Lodge, KS
Musician

Kansas State Map

Kansas River

Manhattan

○

Topeka ✪

Overland Park ○

Kansas City ○

○ Salina

Olathe ○

Smoky Hill River

Flint Hills

Arkansas River

○ Wichita

Kansas State Facts

Population: About 2,688,418

Area: 82,277 square miles (213,096 sq km)

Motto: "Ad Astra per Aspera" ("To the Stars Through Difficulties")

Song: "Home on the Range," words by Brewster Higley and
music by Dan Kelly

23

Index

Web Sites

Due to the changing nature of Internet links, PowerKids Press has developed an online list of Web sites related to the subject of this book. This site is updated regularly. Please use this link to access the list:

www.powerkidslinks.com/amst/ks/